PAPERBACK **PLUS**

Table of Contents

Meet Linda Glaser

LINDA GLASER likes to work in her garden. She sees how worms make the earth better for her plants. Ms. Glaser writes about worms in *50 Simple Things Kids Can Do to Save the Earth* and in *50 Simple Things Kids Can Do to Recycle.*

Meet Loretta Krupinski

LORETTA KRUPINSKI likes to paint pictures of boats, lighthouses, and harbors. She also likes to draw little, soft, fuzzy things!

WONDERFUL WORMS

WONDERFUL WORMS

BY LINDA GLASER
PICTURES BY LORETTA KRUPINSKI

HOUGHTON MIFFLIN COMPANY

BOSTON

ATLANTA   DALLAS   GENEVA, ILLINOIS   PALO ALTO   PRINCETON

TO MY PARENTS,
WHOSE LOVE OF NATURE HAS
OPENED WORLDS TO ME

Acknowledgments

Grateful acknowledgment is made for use of the following material:

Text

1 *Wonderful Worms,* by Linda Glaser, illustrated by Loretta Krupinski. Text copyright © 1992 by Linda Glaser. Illustrations copyright © 1992 by Loretta Krupinski. Reprinted by permission of The Millbrook Press. All rights reserved. **30** "Mirthworms," by Marty Jones, from August/September 1988 *Jack and Jill* magazine. Copyright © 1988 by Mirthworms, Ltd. Reprinted by permission of Perennial Pictures. Cover copyright © 1988 by Children's Better Health Institute, Benjamin Franklin Literary and Medical Society, Inc., Indianapolis, IN. Reprinted by permission. **32** "Glowworm," from *One at a Time,* by David McCord. Copyright © 1961, 1962 by David McCord. Reprinted by permission of Little, Brown and Company.

Illustrations

32 Susan Swan.

Photography

ii Courtesy of Linda Glaser (t); courtesy of Loretta Krupinski (b). **28** © 1994 ZEFA Germany/The Stock Market (l); © 1986 Jeff Lepore/Photo Researchers (r). **28-29** Rob Atkins/The Image Bank (border). **29** © USDA Science Source/Photo Researchers (tl); © Rod Planck/Tony Stone Images (tr); © Stephen Dalton/Photo Researchers (b).

2001 Impression
Houghton Mifflin Edition, 1996
Copyright © 1996 by Houghton Mifflin Company. All rights reserved.

Printed in the U.S.A.

ISBN 0-395-73216-6

10 11 12 13 14 15-B-02 01 00

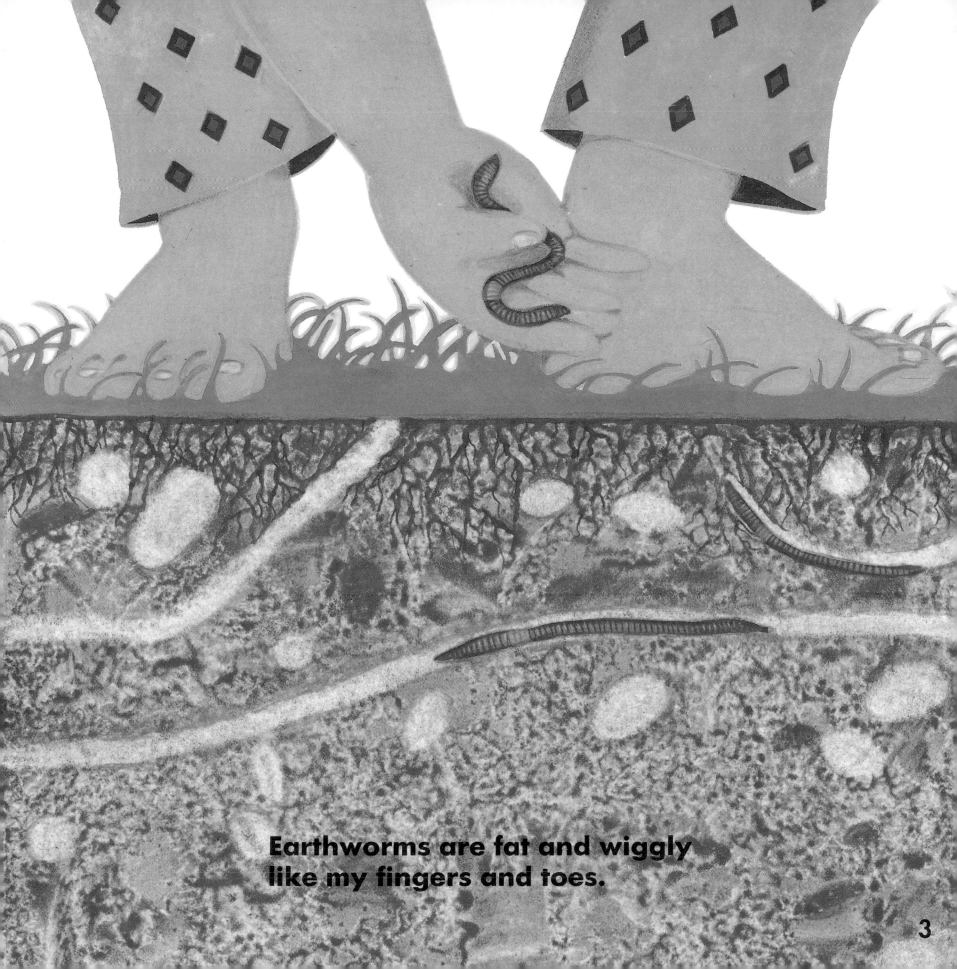

Earthworms are fat and wiggly
like my fingers and toes.

4

They live where it is cool and dark and damp,
where roots spread out like underground trees.

Worms feel sounds with their whole bodies.
They feel thunder when I walk.

They are wonderful diggers.
They dig passageways and burrows.

8

But they don't use shovels
or fingers or toes.

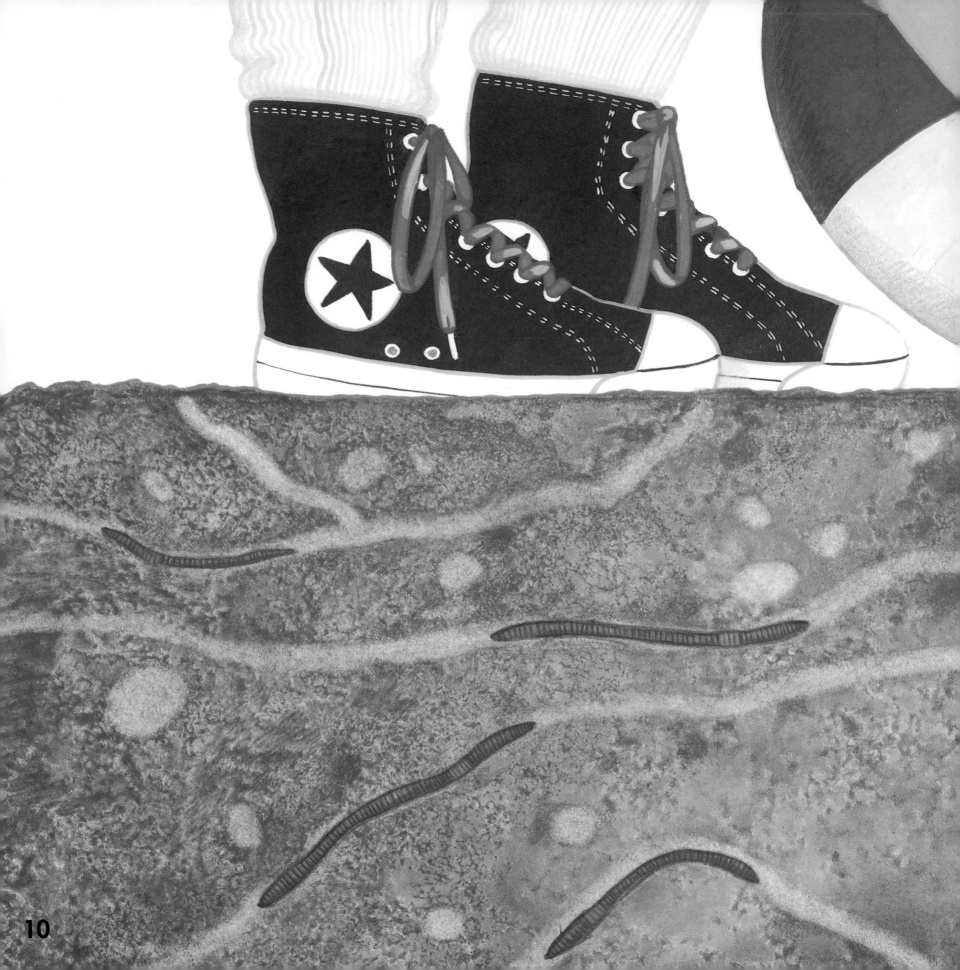

How do they do it?
They eat their way through and move along.

They stretch out, long and thin,
and squeeze in, short and fat.

12

**Stretch and squeeze, stretch and squeeze.
Eat and dig, move and dig.**

Earthworms mix and turn the dirt
as they dig and tunnel in the earth.

15

They make the soil soft and airy
so the roots of plants can breathe and grow.

Worms don't have eyes or ears or a nose.
They do have a mouth.

And they need food, just like I do.
But they eat dirt and rotting leaves.

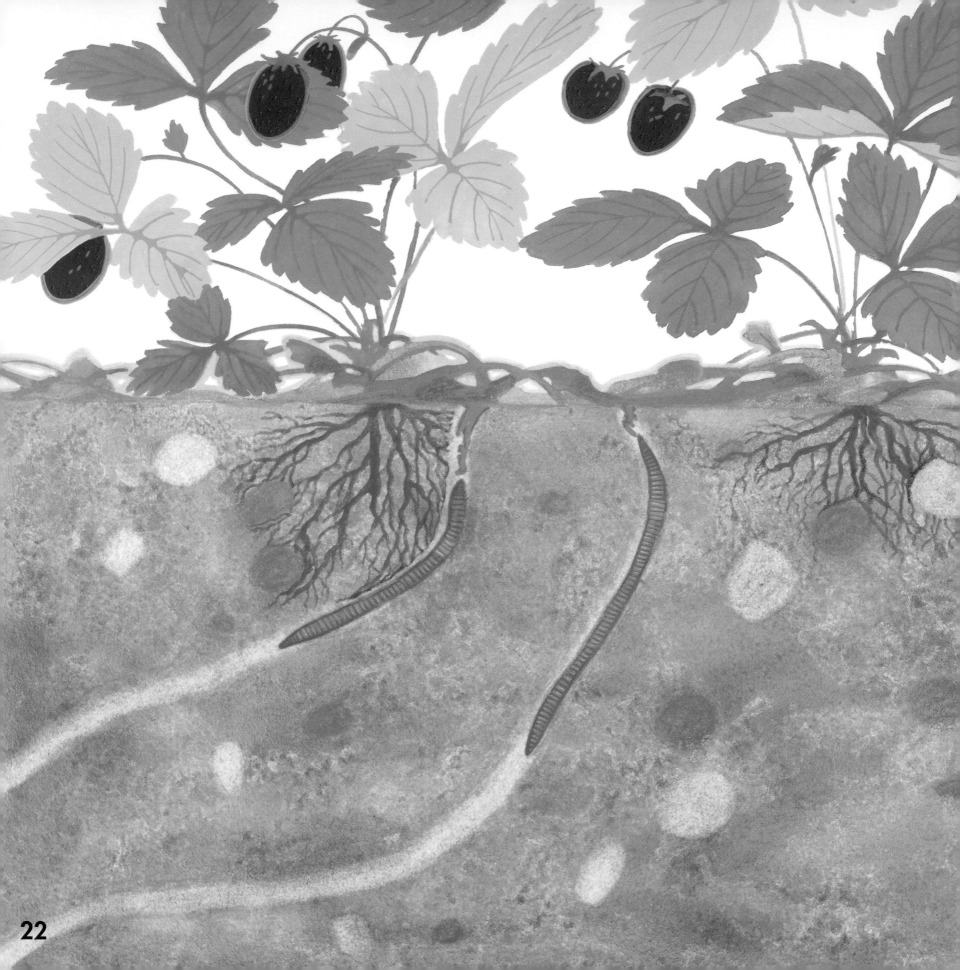

They swallow tiny pieces.
And inside the worms, the food changes.

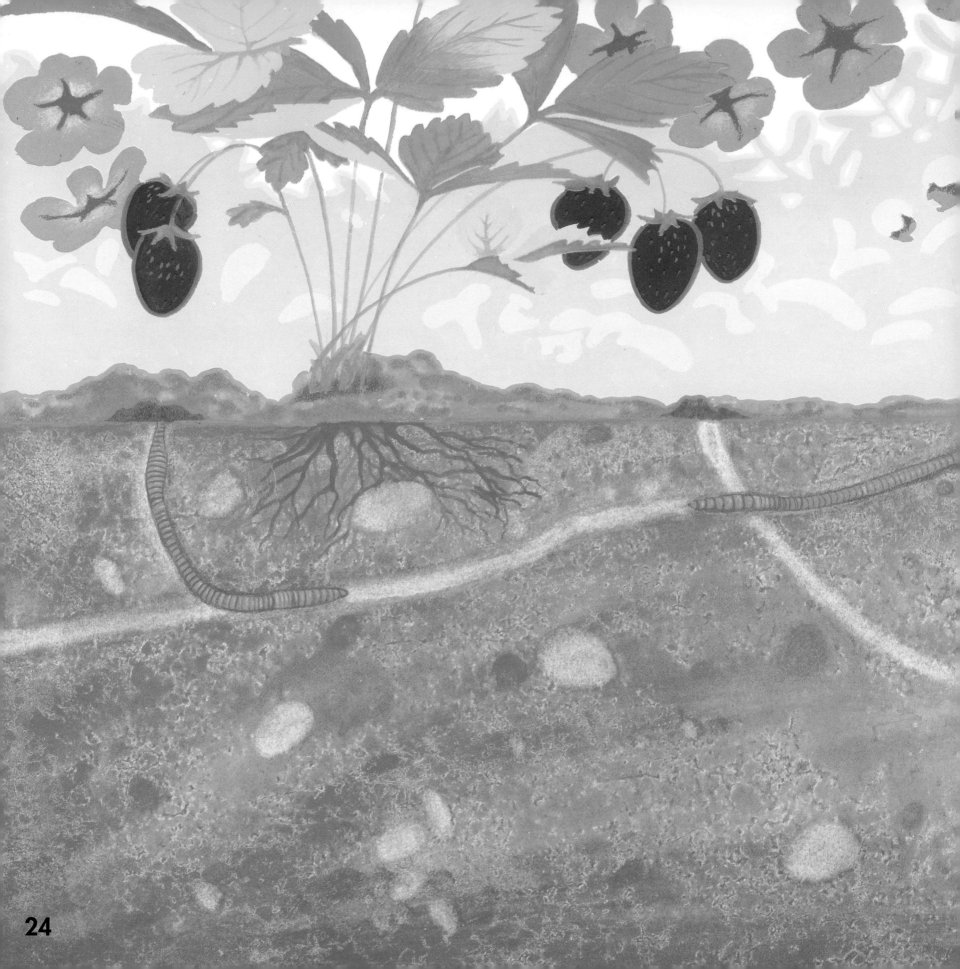

When it comes out of their tail ends,
it makes the earth rich so plants can grow.

**Earthworms are my helpers, the underground gardeners.
We work hard in the dirt in my garden, their home.**

Creepy Crawly Helpers

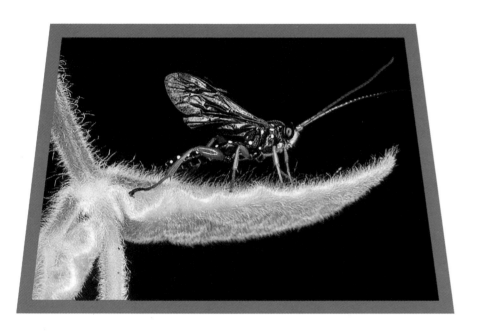

Wasps carry food from plant to plant. Plants need this food to live.

Mole crickets use their legs to loosen soil. This helps plants grow.

Ladybugs help farmers by eating the insects that eat crops.

Beetles keep our world clean by eating dead trees.

Silkworms spin a silk thread. We use this silk to make clothes.

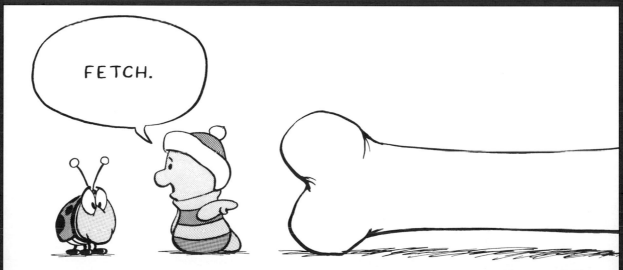

MARTY JONES

Glowworm

Never talk down to a glowworm —
Such as *What do you knowworm?*
How's it down belowworm?
Guess you're quite a slowworm.
No. Just say
   Helloworm!

   by David McCord